The Hans Wilhelm Treasury of Jokes

By
Joseph Rosenbloom

Illustrated by
Hans Wilhelm

STERLING

New York / London

STERLING and the distinctive Sterling logo are registered trademarks of
Sterling Publishing Co., Inc.

Library of Congress Cataloging-in-Publication Data Available

2 4 6 8 10 9 7 5 3 1

This book is a compilation of 5 books originally published by Sterling Publishing Co., Inc.:
THE FUNNIEST JOKE BOOK EVER!, text copyright © 1986 by Joseph Rosenbloom,
illustration copyright © 1986 by Hans Wilhelm
MY FIRST BOOK OF DINOSAUR JOKES, text copyright © 1986 by Joseph Rosenbloom,
illustration copyright © 1986 by Hans Wilhelm, Inc.
MY FIRST BOOK OF KNOCK-KNOCK JOKES, text copyright © 1986 by Joseph Rosenbloom,
illustration copyright © 1986 by Hans Wilhelm, Inc.
THE FUNNIEST HAUNTED HOUSE BOOK EVER!, text copyright © 1989 by Joseph Rosenbloom,
illustration copyright © 1989 by Hans Wilhelm, Inc.
THE FUNNIEST RIDDLE BOOK EVER!, text copyright © 1984 by Joseph Rosenbloom,
illustration copyright © 1984 by Hans Wilhelm, Inc.

Published in 2009 by Sterling Publishing Co., Inc.
387 Park Avenue South, New York, NY 10016
Distributed in Canada by Sterling Publishing
c/o Canadian Manda Group, 165 Dufferin Street
Toronto, Ontario, Canada M6K 3H6
Distributed in the United Kingdom by GMC Distribution Services
Castle Place, 166 High Street, Lewes, East Sussex, England BN7 1XU
Distributed in Australia by Capricorn Link (Australia) Pty. Ltd.
P.O. Box 704, Windsor, NSW 2756, Australia

Printed in China
All rights reserved

Sterling ISBN 978-1-4027-6397-7

For information about custom editions, special sales, premium and
corporate purchases, please contact Sterling Special Sales
Department at 800-805-5489 or specialsales@sterlingpublishing.com.

Chapter 1
Silly Jokes!

Why do bees hum?
Because they don't
know the words.

Why did the elephant quit the circus?

He got tired of working for peanuts.

Which clown has
the biggest shoes?

The one with the
biggest feet.

Why did the chicken cross the playground?

To get to the other slide.

What do you get if you cross a cocker spaniel, a poodle, and a rooster?

Cock-a-poodle-doo!

Why does a chicken stand on one leg?

If it lifted the other leg it would fall down.

Why does a chicken lay an egg?

If she dropped it, it would break.

Is it right to swim on a full stomach?

No, it's better to swim on water.

Why don't fish go away for the summer?

Because they're always in schools.

What cat lives in the ocean?

An octo-puss.

What do two oceans
say when they meet?

Nothing, they just wave.

What's the difference
between a fish and a piano?

You can't tuna fish.

What do you get if you cross
a cow and a duck?

Milk and quackers.

Why do cows wear bells?

Because their horns don't work.

Do cows give milk?

No, you have to take it from them.

Did you know it takes three
sheep to make a sweater?

I didn't even know
they could knit.

What is black and white and blue all over?

A skunk at the North Pole.

What is black and white and green?

A seasick penguin.

What is yellow, then gray, then yellow, then gray?

An elephant rolling down a hill with a daisy in its mouth.

What is black and white and red all over?

A raccoon with diaper rash.

What did the football say to the football player?

I get a kick out of you.

Does your dog have a license?

No, he isn't old enough to drive.

What has four wheels
and flies?

A garbage truck.

What happens when it
rains cats and dogs?

You step into a poodle.

How do you catch a monkey?

Climb up a tree and act
like a banana.

What is a twip?

What a wabbit takes when
it wides a twain.

How do you catch
a squirrel?

Climb up a tree and
act like a nut.

What is long and thin
and goes "Hith, hith"?

A snake with a lisp.

SILLY: I'm going to give my elephant a bath.
WILLY: That must be hard work.
SILLY: No, it's easy. The hard part is getting him into the tub.

FATHER: Why did you put a frog in your little sister's bed?

BILLY: Because I couldn't find a mouse.

How can you tell if there's an elephant in your bed?
Look for peanut shells.

Where do chickens dance?

At the fowl ball.

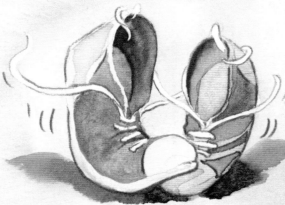

Where do sneakers
dance?

At the football.

Where do cows dance?

At the meatball.

Where do snowflakes dance?

At the snowball.

FIRST SNAKE: I hope I'm not poisonous.
SECOND SNAKE: Why?
FIRST SNAKE: I just bit my tongue.

PARK RANGER: You can't fish here.
BOY: I'm not fishing. I'm taking my worm for a swim.

Where do hogs keep
their money?

In piggy banks.

Where do fish keep
their money?

In river banks.

What is black and white
and has sixteen wheels?

A panda on roller skates.

What's the difference
between an elephant and a
jar of peanut butter?

The elephant doesn't stick to
the roof of your mouth.

Why did the elephant
wear red underwear?

So he could hide in the
strawberry patch.

Why did the elephant
wear green sneakers?

Because his red ones were in
the wash.

Why did the chicken cross the road?

To get to the other side.

Why did the turkey cross the road?

It was the chicken's day off.

Why did the elephant cross the road?

To get to the next chapter of this book!

Chapter 2
Dinosaur Jokes!

Knock-knock.
Who's there?
Dinah.

Dinah who?
Dinah-saur!

NAN: Why are you
snapping your
fingers?
DAN: To keep the
dinosaurs away.

NAN: That's crazy. There
are no dinosaurs
around here.
DAN: See? It works.

What is as big as a dinosaur but
doesn't weigh anything?

The shadow of a dinosaur.

Why do you always find
dinosaurs on the ground?

Because they won't climb trees.

Why did the owl sit on the
dinosaur's head?

Because it didn't give a hoot.

Why did the dinosaur paint
its toenails red?

So that it could hide in the petunias.

Where do dinosaurs go to swim?

To the dino-shore.

What happens when a dinosaur dives into the ocean?

It goes "splash"!

How to you keep a dinosaur
from smelling?

Put a clothespin on its nose.

What happens when
a green dinosaur
goes swimming in
the Red Sea?

It gets wet.

What weighs 50 tons, has
big teeth, and is blue?

A dinosaur holding its breath.

How many dinosaur skeletons can you put into an empty museum?

One. After that the museum isn't empty anymore.

Why don't dinosaurs do well in school?

Because their heads are so empty.

Why do little dinosaurs drink milk?

Because milk is good for bones.

DO NOT
FEED

Why is a dinosaur skeleton like a penny?

Because it has a head on one side and a tail on the other.

How do you make a dinosaur skeleton laugh?

Tickle its funny bone.

What do you call dinosaur skeletons that sleep all day?

Lazybones.

EXIT

When a dinosaur goes into a restaurant, where does it sit?

Anywhere it wants.

How do you make a dinosaur stew?

Keep it waiting two hours.

What always follows a dinosaur out of the restaurant?

Its tail.

What would happen if a
dinosaur sat in front of
you at the movies?

You would miss most
of the show.

What dinosaur eats
popcorn with its tail?

They all do. No dinosaur takes
its tail off to eat popcorn.

What vegetable are you
if a dinosaur sits on you?

Squash.

What has a head
like a dinosaur,
a body like a dinosaur,
a tail like a dinosaur,
looks just like a dinosaur,
but isn't a dinosaur?

A picture of a dinosaur.

What is as big as a
house and has two
legs and six wheels?

A dinosaur on in-line skates.

How do you get a
100-foot-tall dinosaur
into a small car?

Open the sun roof.

How do you get five 100-foot
dinosaurs into a small car?

Put two in the front, two in
the back, and one in the glove
compartment.

How do you run over a dinosaur?

Climb up its neck, run along its back,
and slide down its tail.

**Why didn't the dinosaur
ride a bicycle?**

Because it didn't have a thumb
to ring the bell.

What is 100 feet long and jumps five times a minute?

A dinosaur with hiccups.

How long should a dinosaur's legs be?

Long enough to reach the ground.

What kind of dinosaur
has red spots?

One with measles.

When does a dinosaur see
as well from either end?

When its eyes are closed.

What goes, "Thud,
thud, thud—OUCH!"?

A dinosaur with a sore toe.

Which dinosaur wears the
biggest cowboy hat?

The one with the biggest head.

What do you call
Tyrannosaurus rex
when it wears a cowboy
hat and boots?

Tyrannosaurus Tex.

What kind of dinosaur can you ride in a rodeo?

A Bronco-saurus.

What do you get when you cross Tyrannosaurus rex and a chicken?

Tyrannosaurus pecks.

Who is a little dinosaur's favorite babysitter?

Ty-granny-saurus rex.

What's the hardest thing about learning to ride a dinosaur?

The ground.

Where did the dinosaur
buy its magic markers?

At the dino-store.

Why are dinosaurs big,
green, and scaly?

Because if they were small,
yellow, and fuzzy, they would
be tennis balls.

Why did the dinosaur
paint itself with magic markers?

So it could hide in the crayon box.

Why shouldn't you add 4 plus 4 when you see a Tyrannosaurus rex?

Because if you add 4 plus 4 you might get ate.

What happened when the little dinosaur took the school bus home?

The police made him bring it back.

How can you tell if a dinosaur
is hiding under your bed?

Your nose is close to the ceiling.

Why did the dinosaur
wear red pajamas?

His pink ones were in the wash.

What do you call a
dinosaur that makes
noises when it sleeps?

A dino-snore.

MOTHER: What do you mean by bringing that 100-foot-long dinosaur into your room?

JUNIOR: It's all right, I'm only keeping him overnight.

How can you tell if there is a dinosaur on your bed?

By the big D on his pajamas.

Why are dinosaurs invited to parties?

Because they are tons of fun.

How does a magician
cut a dinosaur in two?

With a dino-saw.

When does a
dinosaur look like a
cute little clown?

When it wears
a cute little
clown suit.

What time is it when you meet Tyrannosaurus rex at a party?

Time to run.

What goes "Ho, ho, ho, ho—PLOP!"?

A dinosaur laughing its head off.

What do you sing to a dinosaur when it's 70 million years old?

"Happy Birthday."

Why did the dinosaur wear dark glasses?

With all these dinosaur jokes, it didn't want to be recognized.

Why did the dinosaur become extinct?

It didn't want to hear any more dinosaur jokes.

Chapter 3

Knock-Knock!

Knock-knock.
  Who's there?
Eddie.
  Eddie who?
Eddie-body home?

Knock-knock.
    Who's there?
Doris.
    Doris who?
Doris a puppy
in the window.

Knock-knock.
    Who's there?
Howard.
    Howard who?
Howard you like to
hold the puppy?

Knock-knock.
    Who's there?
Wooden shoe.
    Wooden shoe who?
Wooden shoe like a
puppy too?

Knock-knock.
    Who's there?
Olive.
    Olive who?
Olive the puppy.

Knock-knock.
      Who's there?
Luke.
      Luke who?
Luke out! There's a hole
in the boat!

Knock-knock.
      Who's there?
Rhoda.
      Rhoda who?
Rhoda boat across the lake.

Knock-knock.
    Who's there?
Dwayne.
    Dwayne who?
Dwayne the lake—
I'm dwowning!

Knock-knock.
    Who's there?
Otto.
    Otto who?
Otto know how to swim.

Knock-knock.
    Who's there?
Jewel.
    Jewel who?
Jewel never find me.

Knock-knock.
    Who's there?
Donahue.
    Donahue who?
Donahue want to
play hide-and-seek?

Knock-knock.
    Who's there?
Freddy.
    Freddy who?
Freddy or not, here
I come!

Knock-knock.
    Who's there?
Stu.
    Stu who?
Stu late to hide.

Knock-knock.
    Who's there?
Ron.
    Ron who?
Ron home!

Knock-knock.
Who's there?
Emma.
Emma who?
Emma 'fraid of the dark.

Knock-knock.
Who's there?
Hugh.
Hugh who?
Hugh go away!

Knock-knock.
  Who's there?
Boo.
  Boo who?
Well, you don't have
to cry about it.

Knock-knock.
  Who's there?
Ivan.
  Ivan who?
Ivan to haunt you.

Knock-knock.
    Who's there?
Hans.
        Hans who?
Hans up!

Knock-knock.
    Who's there?
Holden.
        Holden who?
Holden up the train.

Knock-knock.
    Who's there?
Yah.
    Yah who?
Ride 'em cowboy!

Knock-knock.
    Who's there?
Danielle.
    Danielle who?
Danielle so loud!

Knock-knock.
    Who's there?
Llama.
    Llama who?
Llama Yankee Doodle Dandy!

Knock-knock.
    Who's there?
Lionel.
    Lionel who?
Lionel roar when he sees you!

Knock-knock.
    Who's there?
Ken.
    Ken who?
Ken I give the elephant
a peanut?

Knock-knock.
    Who's there?
Phil.
    Phil who?
Phil like giving him
another one?

Knock-knock.
    Who's there?
Thea.
    Thea who?
Thea later, alligator.

Knock-knock.
    Who's there?
Leif.
    Leif who?
Leif me alone.

Knock-knock.
    Who's there?
Harry.
    Harry who?
Harry up and
open the door!

Knock-knock.
    Who's there?
Adam.
    Adam who?
Adam my way! I'm
coming in!

Knock-knock.
    Who's there?
Omar.
    Omar who?
Omar goodness, what's that?

Knock-knock.
   Who's there?
Les.
   Les who?
Les go for a swim.

Knock-knock.
   Who's there?
Tommy.
   Tommy who?
Tommy ache!

Knock-knock.
Who's there?
Ethan.
Ethan who?
Ethan this a nice picnic?

Knock-knock.
Who's there?
Barbie.
Barbie who?
Barbie-cue chicken!

Knock-knock.
   Who's there?
Sid.
   Sid who?
Sid down in your seat.

Knock-knock.
   Who's there?
Bea.
   Bea who?
Bea-have or you stay
after school.

Knock-knock.
  Who's there?
Oscar.
  Oscar who?
Oscar silly question and
you get a silly answer.

Knock-knock.
  Who's there?
Hutch.
  Hutch who?
Did you sneeze?

Knock-knock.
  Who's there?
Justin.
    Justin who?
Justin time for your party.

Knock-knock.
  Who's there?
Sue.
    Sue who?
Sue-prise!

Knock-knock.
    Who's there?
Abby.
    Abby who?
Abby birthday!

Knock-knock.
    Who's there?
Bertha.
    Bertha who?
Bertha-day cake!

Knock-knock.
  Who's there?
Shirley.
  Shirley who?
Shirley am tired of knock-knock jokes.

Knock-knock.
  Who's there?
Aldo.
  Aldo who?
Aldo anything to get
away from these
knock-knock jokes!

Chapter 4

Spooky Jokes!

What is worse than seeing a ghost?

Seeing two ghosts.

What do you hear when you knock on the door of a haunted house?

"WHOOOOOOO's there?"

What goes around a haunted house but doesn't move?

The fence.

Which monster can jump
higher than a haunted house?

Any monster. A haunted house
can't jump.

Is it true that a monster
won't touch you if you carry
a flashlight?

That depends on how fast
you carry it.

How many vampires does it
take to put in a light bulb?

None. Vampires like the dark.

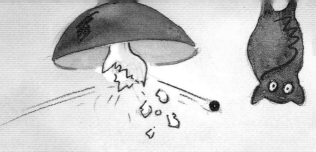

Why did the vampire hit the clock?

Because the clock struck first.

Why do spiders spin webs?

Because they don't know how to knit.

What time is it when five monsters chase after two ghosts?

Five after two.

How does a witch tell time?

With a witch watch.

What does a mother ghost say to a little ghost who talks too much?

"Don't spook until you're spooken to."

How does a monster count to 32?

It takes its shoes off.

Where do lady monsters keep their hands?

In a handbag.

What part of a house makes a mummy nervous?

The living room.

Do mummies ever get presents?

Yes, on Mummy's Day.

Why did the monster put
three ducks in a carton?

He wanted a box of quackers.

What do little
ghosts chew?

Boo-ble gum.

Why can't you join a monster in a glass of milk?

Because there isn't room for both of you in one glass.

What does a monster musician eat for breakfast?

Rock 'n' roll.

What did the monster do in the kitchen?

It beat the eggs, whipped the cream, and battered the fish.

What part of a house does
a mummy like best?

The DIE-ning room.

What scary creature do
you find in a lunch box?

A sand witch.

Which monster eats fried chicken with its fingers?

They all do. No monster takes off its fingers to eat fried chicken.

What is a ghost's favorite lunch?

Spook-ghetti.

What happens when a sandwich sees a ghost?

It becomes a scream cheese and yell-y sandwich.

What game do little ghosts play?

Haunt and shriek.

What is the best way to talk to the Frankenstein monster?

By long distance.

What game do little ghouls play?

Corpse and robbers.

Why was the werewolf invited to the party?

Because he was a howl.

Why was the ghost invited?

Because he was a scream.

Why wasn't the zombie invited?

Because he couldn't be the life of the party.

Why wasn't the vampire invited?

Because he was a pain in the neck.

What do you say when you meet a two-headed monster?

"Hello, hello!"

What do giants like to play at parties?

Swallow the leader.

Why didn't the skeleton go to the party?

Because he had no-body to go with.

What happened when the werewolf fell into the washing machine?

He became a wash-and-wear wolf.

How do you know there is a giant in your dryer?

The door is hard to close.

GARY GHOST: You look dizzy. What happened?
LARRY GHOST: My mother put my sheets in the washing machine. She forgot I was still in them.

What steps would you take when a ghost chases you around a haunted house?

Giant steps.

What kind of ant is 15 feet tall?

A gi-ANT.

What do you do with a blue ghost?

Cheer him up.

What's pink and yellow and goes "Crunch, crunch"?

A monster eating crackers in bed.

What nursery rhyme do little ghosts like to hear?

Little Boo Peep.

In what room do you find the most zombies?

The dead-room.

What do ghosts hunt with?

 What comes out at night and bites people?

A boo and arrow.

A mosquito in a black cape.

What is white, scares people, and jumps?

A ghost who's afraid of ghosts.

What story do little ghouls like to hear before they go to bed?

Ghouldilocks and the Three Scares.

Why did the monster wear
red suspenders?

To keep his
pants up.

What is the difference between
a furry monster and a flea?

A furry monster can have fleas, but
a flea can't have furry monsters.

What do ghouls wear on
their feet when it rains?

Ghoul-oshes.

What do ghosts wear on their feet when it rains?

BOO-ts.

How do you keep a werewolf from ripping out the front seat of a car?

Make him sit in the back.

What is the first thing a ghost does when he gets into a car?

He BOO-ckles his seat belt.

How do witches get around fast?

They fly on their bar-OOOOM sticks.

What did the witch say to the little broom?

"Go to sweep, wittle baby."

Why do witches fly on broomsticks?

Because vacuum cleaners don't have long enough cords.

What is the best safety rule for witches?

"Don't fly off the handle."

What do baby ghosts say when they have to go home?

"BOO-hoo!"

What do two-headed monsters say when they have to go home?

"Bye-bye!"

What does a 100-foot monster say when it has to go home?

"So long!"

Chapter 5

Goofy Riddles!

What do elephants have that no other animals have?

Baby elephants.

What is a baby elephant
after he is six months old?

Seven months old.

How could twelve children and two dogs be under one umbrella and not get wet?

It wasn't raining.

How do you know that carrots are good for the eyes?

Have you ever seen a rabbit wearing eyeglasses?

Why does a cowboy
ride his horse?

Because his horse is too
heavy to carry.

Who goes to bed
with his shoes on?

A horse.

Why do flies walk on ceilings?

If they walked on the floor, someone might step on them.

What is small, purple, and dangerous?

A grape with a six-shooter.

Why do witches fly on broomsticks?

It's better than walking.

Where does an 800-pound gorilla sleep?

Anywhere it wants.

Who was the first animal in space?

The cow that jumped over the moon.

What kind of star wears sunglasses?

A movie star.

What rises in the morning and waves all day?

A flag.

What is black and white and red all over?

A sunburned zebra.

What is big and white and is found on the Equator?

A lost polar bear.

What did the boy octopus say to the girl octopus?

"I want to hold your hand, hand, hand, hand, hand, hand, hand, hand."

Why do lions eat raw meat?

Because they don't know how to cook.

How do you get a mouse to fly?

Buy it an airline ticket.

What is white outside, green inside, and hops?

A frog sandwich.

How can you tell there's an elephant in the refrigerator?

The door won't shut.

What time is it when a monster sits on a chair?

Time to get a new chair.

What do you do
when a monster
sneezes?

Get out of the way!

How do you talk to giants?

Use BIG WORDS!

What is black and yellow and goes "Zzub, zzub"?

A bee going backwards.

What is a grasshopper?

An insect on a pogo stick.

What side of a squirrel has the most fur?

The outside.

What is big and gray and has a red face?

An elephant holding its breath.

Why do postal workers carry letters?

Because the letters can't carry themselves.

Why do firefighters wear red suspenders?

To keep their pants up.

What did the big chimney say to the little chimney?

"You shouldn't smoke."

What has two wheels, two horns, and gives milk?

A cow on a motorcycle.

Why do monkeys
scratch themselves?

Because they're the
only ones who know
where it itches.

Why is an elephant large,
gray, and lumpy?

Because if it were small,
white, and smooth, it would
be an egg.

Why does a giraffe have a long neck?

Because its head is so far from its body.

What is the difference between a mailbox and a kangaroo?

If you don't know, I won't send you out to mail a letter!

What does a 200-pound
mouse say?

"Here, kitty, kitty!"

What sound do two
porcupines make when
they kiss?

"Ouch!"

What did one flea say
to the other flea?

"Shall we walk or take
the dog?"

What is the strongest
animal in the world?

A turtle, because it carries
its house on its back.

What has a hump and sings like a bird?

A camel carrying a canary.

What makes more noise than one squealing pig?

Two squealing pigs.

What do you do with a pickle when it's one year old?

Wish it a happy birthday.

What is yellow and swims underwater?

A yellow submarine.

The End

What goes "Clomp, clomp, clomp, squish"?

An elephant with a wet sneaker.